Dear Grand[ma],

I just wan[t] [to tell you]

I love you a[nd] [you have]

been an influe[nce] on my life. After

your accident and coping with

everything that came after. Being

stricten to a wheelchair for the majority

of your life. You were such a wonder[ful]

mother to my mom. Thank [you so]

much, Grandma. I Lov[e you]

GRANDMA,
Do You Remember When?

*Sharing a Lifetime
of Loving Memories*

PAINTINGS BY
JIM DALY

HARVEST HOUSE PUBLISHERS

EUGENE, OREGON

GRANDMA, *Do You Remember When?*
Text Copyright © 2003 by Harvest House Publishers
Eugene, Oregon 97402
www.harvesthousepublishers.com

ISBN-13: 978-0-7369-1050-7
ISBN-10: 0-7369-1050-6

Artwork Copyright © by Jim Daly and may not be reproduced without permission. For more information about art prints featured in this book, please contact:

  Jim Daly
  P.O. Box 25146
  Eugene, OR 97402
  www.jimdalyart.com

Design and production by Koechel Peterson & Associates, Inc., Minneapolis, Minnesota

Scripture quotations are taken from: the Holy Bible: New International Version®. NIV®. Copyright © 1973, 1978, 1984 by the International Bible Society. Used by permission of Zondervan Publishing House; and the Holy Bible, New Living Translation, copyright ©1996. Used by permission of Tyndale House Publishers, Inc., Wheaton, Illinois 60189, U.S.A. All rights reserved.

Printed in China

 11 12 / IM / 20 19 18 17 16

Grandma, Do You Remember When?

Grandma, do you remember when…
You were a girl so very young?
With dreams and wishes for
A sweet life just begun.

Jump rope, hopscotch, and happy rhymes,
Best friends, peppermint sticks,
Good ol' times.

Years later—children of your own,
Traditions, celebrations,
Home sweet home.

Grandma, do you remember when…
You heard I was on the way?
Did you have dreams and wishes
On my birth day?

Memories, keepsakes passed on to me,
Stories of love
Create your legacy.

Talking, sharing, discovering each other,
I am so very lucky
You are *my* grandmother.

Tell me about your life, Grandma _____

With love,

_____

Grandchildren are the crowning glory of the aged;
parents are the pride of their children.

The Book of Proverbs

Our Family Tree

Grandma, did you have a grandma and grandpa? _____
What were their names? _____

How many brothers and sisters do you have? _____
What are their names and ages? _____
_____

When were your children born? _____
What are their names and birthdates? _____
_____
_____

Where does our family come from originally? _____
_____

Tell me a favorite story about our family... _____
_____
_____
_____
_____
_____

The Day You Were Born

Grandma, when is your birthday? _____

_____

Where were you born? _____

_____

How did your mom and dad pick your name? _____

_____

Who was president when you were born? _____

_____

What was happening in the world when you were born?

_____

_____

_____

_____

It's a pleasure to share one's memories. Everything remembered
is dear, endearing, touching, precious. At least the past is safe—
though we didn't know it at the time. We know it now.
Because it's in the past; because we have survived.

Susan Sontag

Your Mom and Dad

Grandma, tell me about your parents. What were they like?

_____

_____

_____

_____

_____

What are the names of your mom and dad? _____

What is your happiest memory about your mom and dad?

_____

_____

_____

_____

_____

_____

_____

When You Were Little

Grandma, do you remember what your childhood home was like?

_____

_____

What were your favorite/least favorite foods? _____

_____

What could you buy with a dollar? _____

_____

How much did it cost to go to the movies? _____
Did you have chores to do each day? _____

_____

What was your room like as a girl? _____

_____

_____

_____

_____

_____

_____

Grandchildren are God's way of
compensating us for growing old.

Mary H. Waldrip

You are told a lot about your education, but some beautiful, sacred memory, preserved since childhood, is perhaps the best education of all.

Fyodor Dostoyevsky

School Days

*G*randma, do you remember when you were a school girl?
Which schools did you go to? _____

_____

_____

Who was your favorite teacher? _____

_____

What was your favorite subject? _____

_____

Which subject was hardest for you? _____

_____

What kind of activities were you involved in throughout
your school years? _____

_____

_____

_____

_____

_____

_____

_____

What About Grandpa?

Grandma, do you remember when you first saw Grandpa?

What did you do on your first date?

How did Grandpa propose?

What did your parents think about your engagement?

When and where did you get married? What was the wedding like?

Did you have any funny nicknames for each other?

What do you love most about Grandpa?

Share with me some special memories from this time in your life…

*W*here we love is home—home that our feet
may leave, but not our hearts.

Oliver Wendell Holmes, Sr.

Your Young Family

Did you work when you had a family? _____

_____

What did Grandpa do for a living? _____

_____

Where did you make your home? _____

_____

What was my mom/dad like at my age? _____

_____

_____

How did you spend time together as a family? _____

_____

What memories do you hold close to your heart about your
young family? _____

_____

_____

_____

_____

_____

Being a Grandma

Grandma, do you remember when I was born? _____

When were your other grandkids born? _____

How is being a grandmother a fun experience for you? _____

What do you like to do with your grandchildren? _____

What do you want your grandkids to know about you?

The feeling of grandparents for their grandchildren can be expressed this way: "Our children are dear to us; but when we have grandchildren, they seem to be more dear than our children were." You might say that the grandmother falls all over herself to try to show her appreciation for her grandchild. It goes right back to those wishes that were made for them when they were little girls: the wish that they would live to become grandmothers someday.

Henry Old Coyote

Furry Friends

Grandma, what pets did you have as a child? _____

What were their names? _____

_____

Did you take care of animals when you were growing up?

_____

What is your favorite memory of a furry friend? _____

_____

Did you let your children have pets? _____

How Does Your Garden Grow?

Grandma, do you remember when you had your first garden?

_____

_____

What is your favorite flower, Grandma? _____

Who taught you how to take care of plants? _____

If you could give me a garden, what flowers and plants would fill it?
What would we do together in this garden? _____

_____

_____

_____

_____

_____

*𝒯*here is a garden in every childhood, an enchanted place where colors are brighter, the air softer, and the morning more fragrant than ever again.

Elizabeth Lawrence

*T*here is a time for everything, and a season
for every activity under heaven.

The Book of Ecclesiastes

There Is a Season...

What is your favorite season of the year, Grandma? _____

_____

When you played as a child, what was your favorite outdoor activity?

_____

_____

Can you recall the landscapes that surrounded you as a child?

_____

_____

_____

_____

Did you ever make a fort in the woods? A trail in the meadow?
A house among the flower bushes? _____

_____

_____

If you could show me one special place in nature, what would it be?

_____

_____

_____

_____

The Gift of Friends

Who were your friends when you were growing up? _____

_____

Did you have a "best friend"? _____

_____

Were you shy as a young girl or outgoing? _____

How were you a good friend? _____

_____

Grandma, share a story about one of your friends… _____

_____

_____

_____

_____

_____

Perfect love sometimes does not
come 'til the first grandchild.

Welsh Proverb

*For the Lord is good. His unfailing love
continues forever, And his faithfulness
continues to each generation.*

The Book of Psalms

Faith Traditions

Did your family go to church when you were a girl? _____

What was your favorite prayer for bedtime and mealtime? _____
_____
_____

What is your favorite verse or memory from church? _____
_____
_____
_____

Grandma, what is your prayer for me? _____
_____
_____
_____
_____

Happy Times

Tell me about a time when you were really happy. _____

_____

_____

What hobbies or activities have brought you joy over the years?

_____

_____

Share with me a story from your life that still makes you laugh.

_____

_____

_____

_____

What makes you happiest about being a grandmother?

_____

_____

_____

_____

_____

Come, my little children, here are songs for you;
Some are short and some are long, and all, all are new.
You must learn to sing them very small and clear,
Very true to time and tune and pleasing to the ear.

Robert Louis Stevenson

The Games People Play

*W*hat games did you and your friends play? _____

_____

_____

When you were young, which songs and rhymes did you sing?

_____

_____

_____

Did you have a favorite toy? _____

As your children grew up, what games did you play with them?

_____

_____

What game do you want to teach me? _____

_____

_____

_____

_____

_____

Dream a Little Dream

Grandma, do you remember what you dreamed about accomplishing? Have you done it?

_____

_____

_____

_____

When you were in school, what would you daydream about?

_____

_____

On your birthday, when you blow out the candles, what wish comes to mind?

_____

_____

_____

_____

What are your wishes for your children? What is your wish for me, Grandma?

_____

_____

_____

_____

_____

Do not pray for gold and jade and precious things; pray that your children and grandchildren may all be good.

Chinese Proverb

*L*ife has been your art.
You have set yourself to music.
Your days are your sonnets.

Oscar Wilde

Inspiration

Grandma, did your mother teach you a special craft? _____

_____

Did you enjoy painting, drawing, or writing as a girl? _____

_____

What is your favorite color? _____

What kind of art or music inspires you? _____

_____

Is there a painting or poem you would love to show me? _____

_____

_____

_____

_____

What things of beauty do you treasure most? _____

_____

_____

_____

Traditions to Build On

$\mathcal{G}$randma, do you remember when you and your parents celebrated family traditions?

_____

Did you start new traditions when your children were born?

_____

_____

Did your mom and grandma give you special recipes and other family secrets?

_____

_____

Share with me a tradition you hope I pass on to my own children some day…

_____

_____

_____

Each day of our lives we make deposits
in the memory banks of our children.

Charles R. Swindoll

Happy Holidays

*H*ow did you celebrate Easter, Thanksgiving, and Christmas as a girl?

_____

_____

_____

How is music a part of your holiday celebrations? _____

_____

What was your first Thanksgiving with Grandpa like? _____

_____

What do you like to do now during the holidays? _____

_____

_____

What do you want me to know about your favorite holiday, Grandma?

_____

_____

_____

Then and Now

Grandma, do you remember when there weren't computers or cell phones? _____
_____

What are the best changes that have taken place during your lifetime? _____
_____
_____
_____

What do you miss about the old days? _____
_____
_____
_____

In what way was your childhood a lot different than mine?
_____
_____

How was it similar? _____
_____
_____
_____
_____

Through my grandmother's eyes I can see more clearly
the way things used to be, the way things ought to be,
and most important of all, the way things really are.

Ed Cunningham

So if you have a grandma,
Thank the good Lord up above,
And give grandma hugs and kisses,
For grandmothers are to love.

Lois Wyse

The Legacy of Keepsakes

$\mathcal{D}$o you have something special that belonged to your
mother or father? _____

_____

Tell me a story about a keepsake that is in our family, Grandma.

_____

_____

Where do you keep photographs or images from your lifetime?
What is your favorite photograph? _____

_____

Did you ever keep a journal? What did you like to record? _____

_____

_____

Memories are special family treasures. What memories about your
parents, children, and life do you want me to hold close to my heart?

_____

_____

_____

_____

_____

A Letter from Grandma

Grandma, what would you want me to know most of all?

Thou knowest not that a glance of thine
Can bring back long departed years
And that thy blue eyes' magic shine
Can overflow my own with tears,
And that each feature soft and fair
And every curl of golden hair,
Some sweet remembrance bears.

Just then thou didst recall to me
A distant long forgotten scene,
One smile, and one sweet word from thee
Dispelled the years that rolled between;
I was a little child again,
And ever after joy and pain
Seemed never to have been.

Anne Brontë

I share these memories with my precious grandchild,

_____

With love,

_____